I0701589

NEURO LINGUISTIC PSYCHOTHERAPY

A Complete Guide For Navigating Emotions And Unlocking The Mind's Potential For Healing And Growth

WALTER ZYAIRE

© [Walter Zyaire] [2024]. All rights reserved.

No part of this book may be reproduced, stored in a retrieval system, or transmitted in any form or by any means, electronic, mechanical, photocopying, recording, or otherwise, without the express written permission of the author, with the exception of small extracts in critical reviews or articles.

DISCLAIMER

The information in this book is intended only for general informational purposes; it should not be used in lieu of professional advice or medical care. Since the author is not licensed to practice therapy, the information offered should not be used in place of the expertise, judgment, or guidance of qualified mental health or medical professionals. Readers are encouraged to consult therapists, medical specialists, or other qualified authorities regarding their particular situation and needs. The publisher and author disclaim all liability for any actions or decisions taken by readers based on the information in this book. Results may vary from person to person and this book's approaches, procedures, and strategies may not be suitable in all circumstances. Considering unique situations and consulting a qualified expert are essential when choosing the right course of action. Neither the publisher nor the author recommend or guarantee the efficacy of any therapy or treatment that is indicated in this book. Because the information is based on the author's research and understanding at the time of publishing, it could not reflect the most recent developments or practices in the treatment area. The publisher and the author both disclaim all liability for the accuracy, completeness, or use of the material in this book. Readers bear full responsibility for the decisions and actions they choose in light of the information presented in this book.

TABLE OF CONTENTS

ABOUT THE BOOK

In the field of psychotherapy, the book "Neuro-linguistic Psychotherapy" is highly influential as it offers a thorough and detailed examination of the fundamentals and practical uses of Neuro-linguistic Programming (NLP). The goal and scope of the book are described in the introduction, along with the target readership and a note of appreciation for all who helped with its creation.

The basics of Neuro-linguistic Psychotherapy are laid out, which also explores the history of NLP, its key ideas, and the fusion of psychology, neurology, and linguistics. This lays the groundwork for a deep comprehension of the topic.

The neurological underpinnings of NLP are explored, which looks at pertinent brain structures and functions. The topic of discussion includes the psychobiology of learning and change, as well as neuroplasticity and its consequences.

This book acts as a vital link between NLP's theoretical foundations and real-world applications.

Language and communication—two essential NLP components—take center stage. This section explores the significance of linguistic patterns, presents the Milton Model and Meta-Model, and offers suggestions for productive communication techniques. These components serve as the basis for the therapeutic methods that are covered later in the book.

The emphasis switches to NLP presuppositions and belief systems. The presuppositions of NLP are understood by readers, as is their function in psychotherapy. The book also looks at ways to change limiting beliefs, highlighting how NLP can change cognitive frameworks in a revolutionary way.

The book covers anchoring and its applications, visual, auditory, and kinesthetic representational systems, and the role of submodalities in altering perceptions, is centered around NLP approaches.

This useful manual gives therapists a wide range of tools to help promote good transformation.

The use of NLP in clinical settings is examined in more detail. Case studies are provided to show how NLP can be integrated with conventional therapy procedures. The ethical aspects of NLP practice are emphasized, with a focus on the proper application of these methods in various clinical contexts.

It examines cognitive restructuring and reframing strategies in the context of NLP. This part covers the process of reframing negative thought patterns, presents cognitive-behavioral approaches, and highlights how NLP interventions can improve emotional well-being.

A specific focus on NLP and trauma resolution is given. The book highlights the importance of NLP in fostering resilience, clarifies the NLP perspective on trauma understanding, and offers trauma resolution procedures. When it comes to handling complicated therapeutic issues, this book is very pertinent.

The book looks ahead covering new developments in NLP research and trends. It draws attention to developments, breakthroughs, and the changing face of NLP treatment. The book also discusses the chances and difficulties that lie ahead, encouraging readers to think about how the profession is constantly changing.

CHAPTER ONE

OVERVIEW OF NEURO- LINGUISTIC PSYCHOTHERAPY

SYNOPSIS OF NEURO-LINGUISTIC COUNSELING

At the nexus of languages, neurology, and psychology, neuro-linguistic psychotherapy (NLP) provides a thorough method for comprehending and promoting positive change in people. This therapy approach is based on a thorough examination of the complex relationships that exist between language, cognition, and behavior. One can understand the tenets and basic ideas that serve as the cornerstone of this dynamic psychotherapy approach by studying the NLP foundations.

BASICS OF PSYCHOLINGUISTIC NEUROLINGUISTIC THERAPY

The fundamental tenet of neuro-linguistic psychotherapy is that people create their own subjective experiences according to their worldviews. NLP is a flexible framework that was developed in the 1970s by Richard Bandler and John Grinder. It incorporates elements of various psychological theories, such as behavioral and cognitive models. It highlights the importance of sensory perception, language patterns, and the influence of neurological processes on behavior.

KNOWING NLP AND HOW IT HAS CHANGED

The development of neuro-linguistic psychotherapy is closely linked to its comprehension of human behavior and communication. Originally intended to be a collection of methods and strategies gleaned from studying outstanding therapists, NLP has developed into a complete psychotherapy strategy.

Its scope and efficacy have been enhanced over time by the integration of ideas from other disciplines, such as systems theory, linguistics, and cybernetics. The way that NLP has evolved is a testament to its flexibility and dedication to being relevant in the dynamic field of psychotherapy.

FUNDAMENTALS AND CENTRAL IDEAS

Numerous fundamental ideas and tenets form the basis of neuro-linguistic psychotherapy and serve as guidelines for its application. One way to improve emotional well-being is through "mapping across," which is the process of transferring favorable sensations from one environment to another.

Another key idea is anchoring, which investigates the relationship between external stimuli and emotional reactions and offers a method for controlling emotions. These ideas, along with others like perceptual positions and reframing, support NLP's holistic approach to addressing the complex interactions between language, neuroscience, and psychology.

COMBINING NEUROLOGY, PSYCHOLOGY, AND LINGUISTICS

To provide a synergistic approach to understanding and influencing human behavior, neuro-linguistic psychotherapy uniquely merges the fields of linguistics, neurology, and psychology. As a component, linguistics explores language patterns and highlights the significance of both verbal and nonverbal communication. The neurological component investigates how our brains create our subjective experiences and interpret information. The third pillar, psychology, offers an understanding of human emotion, cognition, and behavior. NLP practitioners can negotiate the complexities of the human mind and promote positive transformation and personal growth because of the smooth integration of different disciplines.

It should be noted that neuro-linguistic psychotherapy is a dynamic and integrative method that goes beyond conventional therapeutic bounds.

CHAPTER TWO

NEURO-LINGUISTIC PSYCHOTHERAPY'S BASIS

KNOWING NLP AND HOW IT HAS CHANGED

An all-encompassing, multidisciplinary approach to comprehending human behavior, communication, and subjective experience is represented by neuro-linguistic psychotherapy or NLP. NLP is a strong toolkit and set of techniques that evolved from the combined work of Richard Bandler and John Grinder in the 1970s, to examine the connections between psychology, linguistics, and neurology. The fundamental tenet of NLP is the conviction that there is a methodical relationship between learned behavioral patterns, language patterns, and brain functions.

The modeling methods used by Bandler and Grinder, who first observed and imitated the behavior and communication patterns of outstanding therapists like Milton Erickson (hypnotherapy), Fritz Perls (Gestalt therapy), and Virginia Satir (family therapy), are credited with helping to develop NLP. Bandler and Grinder created a framework that could be used in psychotherapy as well as other areas of personal and professional growth by taking apart the fundamental structures and tactics of these therapeutic techniques.

FUNDAMENTALS AND CENTRAL IDEAS

Several fundamental ideas form the basis of NLP and provide conceptual frameworks for its use in psychotherapy. The notion that people create their subjective reality based on their worldview is one of the fundamental tenets.

Language, cognitive functions, and sensory perception all influence our subjective experience. NLP proposes that people may modify their perceptions and reactions, resulting in beneficial changes in behavior and emotional well-being, by comprehending and acting upon these subjective experiences.

The importance of choice and flexibility is one of NLP's core concepts. NLP acknowledges that people can become mired in ineffective thought and behavior patterns. NLP seeks to increase a person's range of responses, enabling more flexibility and the capacity to select more adaptive behaviors, by investigating behavioral patterns, belief systems, and brain mechanisms. The humanistic and client-centered pillars of psychotherapy are in line with this emphasis on giving people the power to make deliberate decisions.

COMBINING NEUROLOGY, PSYCHOLOGY, AND LINGUISTICS

The unique combination of languages, neurology, and psychology that distinguishes NLP from conventional treatment modalities. NLP heavily relies on linguistics since it studies the patterns of language people use to speak with each other and with themselves. NLP practitioners have the power to influence and transform cognitive processes, which in turn affect emotions and actions, by comprehending and changing language patterns.

In Natural Language Processing (NLP), neurology is the study of how the brain creates thinking and behavior patterns and analyzes information. NLP professionals examine the neural underpinnings of perception, memory, and learning to recognize and alter deeply ingrained habits that might be a factor in psychological suffering. This neurological viewpoint makes it possible to design focused interventions that can remodel dysfunctional brain connections and promote constructive development.

NLP's integration of psychology entails investigating psychological frameworks and processes to comprehend how people see and interpret their experiences. NLP is a practical and action-oriented methodology that adapts and synthesizes findings from multiple psychological theories. The goal of NLP's psychological dimension is to offer practical solutions for a variety of psychological issues.

CHAPTER THREE

THE NLP'S NEUROLOGICAL FOUNDATION

BRAIN FUNCTIONS AND STRUCTURES RELATED TO NLP

The complex relationship between brain functions and structures is explored in The Neurological Basis of Neuro-Linguistic Programming (NLP), which offers insights into how neural processes form the foundation of NLP. Examining the areas of the brain connected to language and communication is one important component.

Language production is greatly influenced by Broca's area in the left frontal cortex, while language comprehension is greatly influenced by Wernicke's region in the left temporal lobe. Knowing how these areas interact is essential to understanding the neurological underpinnings of NLP's successful communication techniques.

NEUROPLASTICITY: A LOOK AT WHAT IT MEANS

NLP is significantly impacted by neuroplasticity, a key idea in the study of the brain's flexibility. This phenomenon describes the brain's ability to rearrange itself throughout life by creating new neural connections. According to neuroplasticity, people can improve their language and cognitive processes by intentionally reshaping their neural networks. This is relevant to NLP.

The aforementioned flexibility highlights the possibility of personal growth and skill development, which is consistent with the fundamental principles of NLP, which stress the malleability of human behavior and cognition.

THE PSYCHOBIOLOGY OF CHANGE AND LEARNING

The neurological foundations of NLP are further explained by the psychobiology of learning and change.

According to NLP, people can intentionally intervene to change their thoughts and behavior patterns. Reinforcing good changes is mostly dependent on the brain's reward system, which is primarily controlled by regions such as the nucleus accumbens and the production of neurotransmitters like dopamine. Using strategies that activate reward pathways, aid in the consolidation of desirable behaviors, and support successful learning and transformation, NLP procedures make use of this psychobiological framework.

An extensive grasp of the neurological foundation of NLP can be obtained by investigating the complex relationships between brain architecture, neuroplasticity, and the psychobiology of learning and transformation. By dissecting these ideas, professionals, and hobbyists can discover how NLP complements the natural abilities of the brain and provide scientific evidence for the benefits of NLP techniques in promoting learning, communication, and personal growth.

CHAPTER FOUR

NLP'S LANGUAGE AND COMMUNICATION

LANGUAGE NORMS AND THEIR INFLUENCE

Natural Language Processing (NLP) relies heavily on language patterns to shape comprehension and communication. These patterns affect how information is communicated and perceived by encompassing the syntax, semantics, and structure of language. Distinct linguistic patterns can affect perceptions, elicit different emotional reactions, and have an impact on how decisions are made. By deciphering and evaluating these patterns, NLP systems can better analyze language by enabling machines to comprehend the subtleties of human communication.

Examining components like sentence structures, word selections, and contextual meanings is all part of the process of studying language patterns. For example, a message's sentiment can be greatly influenced by the language used, whether it is good or negative.

NLP algorithms can extract sentiment, detect tone, and understand the underlying emotions in text data by recognizing and analyzing these patterns. Furthermore, identifying language patterns helps to build more complex language models that can produce replies that are coherent and appropriate for the given situation.

MILTON MODEL AND META-MODEL

The Milton Model and the Meta-Model are two different NLP frameworks that shed light on communication patterns and language structure. By recognizing and addressing linguistic tendencies that could result in misconceptions or imprecise communication, the Meta-Model focuses on accuracy and clarification. It places a strong emphasis on crafting targeted inquiries that will provide more in-depth answers and improve communication clarity. Implementing the Meta-Model in NLP helps improve language processing algorithms, resulting in responses that are more contextually appropriate and better understand user input.

On the other hand, the Milton Model, which bears Milton Erickson's name, investigates the skill of employing language to create trance-like experiences and encourage flexible thinking. To enable people to investigate their interpretations and produce subjective meanings, this approach purposefully uses ambiguity, presuppositions, and ambiguous terminology. Understanding and applying Milton Model components in NLP can improve the conversational AI system's ability to generate language naturally and adaptably, leading to more interesting and flexible interactions.

SUCCESSFUL COMMUNICATION TECHNIQUES

Successful interactions revolve around effective communication, and natural language processing (NLP) attempts to imitate and improve this feature of human communication in robots. In NLP applications, a variety of tactics support efficient communication. Context awareness is an important component, where models are made to comprehend and react according to the conversation's context. Creating responses that are appropriate and cohesive, entails taking into account prior messages as well as the general dialogue flow.

Sentiment analysis, which entails identifying and interpreting the emotions portrayed in the text, is another crucial tactic. Responses that are responsive to the conversation's emotional tone can be provided by NLP models that are trained to recognize sentiment in user input. Furthermore, NLP systems that integrate feedback loops and learning mechanisms can continuously enhance user satisfaction and communication accuracy.

Language patterns, the Milton Model, and the Meta-Model are fundamental ideas in NLP that influence how computers comprehend and produce communication that resembles that of humans. NLP systems can be further enhanced by employing effective communication tactics, which can help them become more emotionally intelligent, context-aware, and flexible in a variety of conversational contexts.

CHAPTER FIVE

BELIEF SYSTEMS AND PRESUPPOSITIONS

EXAMINATION OF NLP HYPOTHESES

The basic tenets of Neuro-Linguistic Programming (NLP) serve as the foundation for this psychological approach's structure. These presumptions are helpful assumptions that, when accepted, can support interpersonal and personal transformation rather than being offered as indisputable facts. "The map is not the territory," according to one such premise, highlights the subjectivity of our experiences and views.

According to NLP, our perceptions of reality are not the same as the actual, objective reality, which emphasizes the significance of appreciating and comprehending different points of view.

The idea that people should not be defined only by their actions is emphasized by another fundamental tenet of NLP: "People are not their behaviors."

Behaviors are viewed as exterior expressions that are influenced by a multiplicity of interior causes. In therapeutic contexts, this premise promotes empathy and understanding and a nonjudgmental approach.

The premise that "Every behavior has a positive intention" pushes people to consider the deeper reasons for their choices. According to NLP, even behaviors that appear to be undesirable might have good intentions behind them, which encourages practitioners to identify and work with these intentions. This assumption fosters empathy by seeking to find positive answers instead of just fixing outward manifestations of behavior.

BELIEF SYSTEMS' FUNCTION IN PSYCHOTHERAPY

Belief systems are essential to the field of psychotherapy because they have a significant influence on how people perceive the world and behave.

These systems act as a lens through which people understand and make sense of the world. They are the result of a confluence of cultural influences, personal experiences, and social standards. Comprehending and tackling these belief systems is essential in psychotherapy to enable significant transformation.

Beliefs can empower or limit people, affecting how they respond to opportunities and problems. Limiting beliefs can impede personal development and well-being. They are frequently engrained as a result of prior traumas or unpleasant experiences. The goal of psychotherapy is to dismantle these limiting ideas by examining their sources and contesting their veracity. Through recognition and adjustment of these beliefs, people can develop a more flexible and optimistic outlook, building resilience and improving their capacity to handle the challenges of life.

Establishing a secure space for people to examine and reassess their belief systems is a crucial part of the therapeutic process.

To assist clients in identifying and changing harmful ideas, therapists use a variety of modalities, including mindfulness exercises, cognitive-behavioral treatments, and narrative therapy. Psychotherapy helps people restructure their belief systems to better reflect their values and goals by raising awareness and providing alternative viewpoints.

TECHNIQUES TO CHANGE LIMITING BELIEFS

A key component of psychotherapy interventions and personal growth is the modification of limiting beliefs. Several tactics can be used to speed up this process of transformation. One such method is cognitive restructuring, which entails recognizing and changing erroneous or skewed thinking. People can change their cognitive habits and make room for more constructive and positive thinking by questioning and rephrasing unfavorable beliefs.

Another method for overcoming limiting beliefs is narrative therapy.

Therapists can help individuals reshape their narratives to support resilience and self-empowerment by looking at the tales they tell themselves about their experiences. This technique entails looking at things from different angles, highlighting your strengths, and rephrasing obstacles as chances to improve.

Limiting beliefs may also be changed by using mindfulness techniques like awareness training and meditation. By practicing present-moment awareness, people can watch their ideas without passing judgment, which frees up conscious choices and lessens instinctive reactions to unfavorable views.

By practicing mindfulness, people can break free from negative thought patterns and adopt a more welcoming and receptive mindset toward their inner sensations.

Investigating NLP tenets, comprehending belief systems' function in psychotherapy, and putting limiting belief-shifting techniques into practice all support the larger goal of psychological health and personal development.

In the context of therapy, these ideas come together to provide helpful understandings and strategies for people who are trying to make sense of the complex relationship between ideas, beliefs, and actions.

CHAPTER SIX

NLP METHODS IN COUNSELING

APPLICATIONS OF ANCHORING

A key idea in Neuro-Linguistic Programming (NLP) with important therapeutic applications is anchoring. When we talk about anchoring, we're talking about the process of connecting a certain stimulus or trigger to a certain emotional or psychological state. Therapists can assist clients reach desired states and control unwanted ones by using anchoring.

A therapist might, for example, assist a client in creating a positive anchor by connecting a particular touch, phrase, or gesture to a confident or serene mood. The anchor helps the client reach and sustain the desired emotional state in difficult circumstances by being reinforced and used repeatedly.

KINESTHETIC, AURAL, AND VISUAL REPRESENTATIONAL SYSTEMS

The representational systems that are visual, aural, and kinesthetic are essential elements of NLP and are critical to psychotherapy. The main sensory modalities that people use to receive and process information are represented by these systems. Therapists can customize therapies for their clients in therapy by having a thorough understanding of their dominant representational system.

Auditory people tend to rely on words and sounds, kinesthetic people on feelings and experiences, and visual people on visual clues and visuals. Therapists can improve communication and more effectively engage with their clients' experiences by matching therapy procedures with their preferred systems, which can lead to a deeper understanding and connection.

SUBMODALITIES AND ADAPTIVE MINDSETS

Submodalities are the more subtle differences that exist within each representational system and have an impact on how people encode and interpret data. Investigating submodalities in psychotherapy can be helpful in modifying emotional reactions and perceptions. For instance, a therapist might collaborate with a client to change the submodalities connected to a painful experience to lessen the emotional impact of that memory. Therapists can help clients undergo significant changes in their subjective experience, which can result in more adaptable and constructive viewpoints, by making little alterations to features like the size, color, or distance of mental representations.

A thorough examination of the sensory elements that underlie a client's experiences is necessary to modify perceptions through submodalities. Therapists assist their clients in dissecting the minute aspects of their mental models and push them to pinpoint the components that are causing them discomfort or constraint. Clients become aware of their perceptions' malleability and the possibility of revolutionary transformation through this process. People can remodel their internal representations, increasing resilience and good emotional experiences, by methodically modifying submodalities.

Key NLP ideas with a variety of therapeutic applications include anchoring, submodalities, and representational systems in the visual, auditory, and kinesthetic domains. By using these strategies, therapists empower their patients by improving communication, assisting with emotion management, and changing self-limiting beliefs. Customized therapeutic interventions are made possible by a knowledge of representational systems, while anchoring offers an organized method of associating stimuli with particular states. Conversely, submodalities provide a more sophisticated method of altering perceptions, allowing clients to reinterpret their experiences and develop more flexible reactions.

CHAPTER SEVEN

UTILIZATIONS IN MEDICAL ENVIRONMENTS

CASE STUDIES OF NATURAL LANGUAGE PROCESSING (NLP) IN PSYCHOTHERAPY

NLP has become a useful tool in the field of psychotherapy, providing insights and applications that improve therapeutic processes. NLP can improve communication between therapists and clients, as demonstrated by case studies examining its incorporation within psychotherapy settings. For example, therapists might learn more about a client's mental processes, emotional states, and behavioral patterns by examining language patterns and linguistic clues. These case studies illustrate how NLP can be used to more effectively identify and address underlying issues in real-world circumstances, resulting in more individualized and targeted therapy interventions.

COMBINING NLP WITH CONVENTIONAL METHODS

One promising way to raise the overall efficacy of psychological interventions is to combine NLP with conventional therapeutic techniques. Conventional psychotherapy techniques frequently focus on oral exchanges and client story analysis. Advanced language analysis is a tool that therapists can add to their repertoire in conjunction with NLP approaches to help them find subtle nuances and obtain a more thorough grasp of their client's experiences. The integration of NLP with conventional methods creates a comprehensive therapy setting where therapists can customize interventions based on a deeper comprehension of the mental and emotional processes of their clients. Therapists can develop a more dynamic and adaptable framework that meets the various requirements of their clients by integrating these approaches.

ETHICAL ISSUES IN THE PRACTICE OF NLP

To ensure appropriate and respectful use of this technology, a detailed assessment of ethical implications is necessary when applying NLP in therapeutic settings. Practitioners have to deal with concerns about permission, privacy, and handling sensitive data responsibly. The possible power imbalances brought about by modern technology in therapy are also a source of ethical concern, underscoring the necessity of striking a balance between technological advancement and the fundamentals of client-centered care. Protecting clients' autonomy and well-being in psychotherapy requires establishing explicit rules for the ethical use of NLP. This entails continuing conversations within the mental health community to develop standards and best practices that give ethical issues top priority while maximizing the potential of NLP to improve therapeutic outcomes.

CHAPTER EIGHT

COGNITIVE REORGANIZATION AND REINTERPRETATION

COGNITIVE BEHAVIORAL APPROACHES IN NLP

To encourage beneficial behavioral changes, cognitive restructuring, a crucial component of cognitive behavioral techniques (CBT) in neuro-linguistic programming (NLP), focuses on recognizing and modifying unfavorable thought patterns. This therapeutic method seeks to reframe faulty cognitions that may contribute to emotional distress or maladaptive actions, acknowledging the interconnection of thoughts, feelings, and behaviors.

Cognitive restructuring, as used in NLP, is the analysis and adjustment of the language and internal representations people use to process information. Through an awareness of the language and cognitive patterns that shape perception, professionals can help people develop more positive thought patterns.

This supports the NLP idea that the words and mental representations we construct influence our subjective experience and serve as a basis for modifying unfavorable cognitive habits.

NEGATIVE THOUGHT PATTERNS REFRAMED

In the framework of cognitive restructuring, reframing negative thought patterns entails changing viewpoints to see things in a more balanced or positive way. Reframing uses linguistic tools to change the meaning associated with thoughts, and NLP techniques highlight the role that language plays in forming our reality.

For example, changing self-limiting thoughts into powerful affirmations might alter one's emotional state and behavior. Practitioners frequently help people recognize cognitive distortions, including catastrophizing or black-and-white thinking, and then work together to reframe those distortions for a more positive outlook.

One of the main objectives of cognitive restructuring and reframing in the context of NLP is to improve emotional well-being. People can see an improvement in their emotional states by confronting and changing problematic thought patterns. This method entails raising awareness of automatic ideas, disproving false beliefs, and swapping them out for more useful and adaptable ones. Deeper emotional transformation can be facilitated by incorporating NLP techniques like metaphorical language and anchoring good emotions. The ultimate goal is to enable people to successfully control their emotions and develop a more resilient and upbeat attitude in life.

NLP's Cognitive Behavioral Techniques provide a strong framework for rethinking problematic thought patterns and cognitive restructuring. NLP's integration of language and cognitive methods is in line with the fundamentals of CBT, giving people the skills they need to improve their emotional health.

Cognitive restructuring in the context of NLP becomes a dynamic process of modifying perceptions, developing positive beliefs, and ultimately contributing to a more positive and adaptable psychological experience through cooperative efforts between practitioners and clients.

CHAPTER NINE

TRAUMA RESOLUTION AND NLP

COMPREHENDING TRAUMA FROM AN NLP ANGLE

Within the field of Neuro-Linguistic Programming (NLP), trauma is viewed from multiple perspectives that include language usage, behavioral reactions, and brain functions. According to NLP theory, trauma is the result of a complex interaction between language representations, cognitive interpretations, and sensory experiences. NLP acknowledges that traumatic experiences can become ingrained in a person's neurology, resulting in reaction patterns that last much beyond the original incident.

According to NLP, traumatic memories are retained in the mind along with particular language and sensory elements, forming what is referred to as an "internal representation." An individual's ideas, feelings, and actions can be influenced by these strong, emotionally charged internal representations. To help people overcome trauma, NLP practitioners try to comprehend and reinterpret these representations.

METHODS FOR RESOLVING TRAUMA

Reprogramming the mind's reaction to traumatic memories is at the heart of NLP's array of trauma resolution tools. By associating helpful or positive feelings with particular events, a strategy known as "anchoring" enables people to access these states in response to traumatic triggers. Reframing is another tactic that helps lessen the emotional impact of painful memories by changing the meaning and interpretation associated with them.

NLP's central idea of submodality is frequently applied to trauma resolution. Practitioners alter the internal representation of traumatic events by interacting with the sensory elements of memories, including sounds, sensations, and visual imagery. People can change the emotional charge and lessen the distress connected to the trauma by changing the submodalities connected to a memory.

A specialist NLP technique called Timeline Therapy addresses the time aspect of memories to resolve trauma. By using this method, professionals assist people in going back over and reframing previous experiences, which helps them rearrange their internal timeline and fosters a more powerful viewpoint.

DEVELOPING RESILIENCE USING NLP

NLP focuses on improving a person's mental and emotional resources, which makes a substantial contribution to the process of creating resilience. Finding and using positive anchors—which link empowered feelings and states to certain cues—is a crucial component.

This makes it possible for people to enter these states whenever they want, which promotes inner strength and resilience under trying circumstances.

NLP linguistic patterns are essential for developing resilience. People are helped to reframe their internal dialogue and self-talk through language strategies, which encourage an optimistic and solution-focused outlook. Through the development of a robust language foundation, NLP enables people to face challenges with a more flexible and self-assured perspective.

NLP also highlights how important it is to set an example of effective actions and tactics. Through seeing and modeling the actions of resilient people, one might learn to take comparable stances when dealing with life's obstacles. NLP strategies, like modeling, give people a useful way to create and incorporate robust thought and behavior patterns.

CHAPTER TEN

PROSPECTS FOR NLP PSYCHOTHERAPY IN THE FUTURE

NEW DIRECTIONS AND STUDIES IN NLP PSYCHOANALYSIS

Technological improvements and a better knowledge of the human mind are driving a wave of new trends and research in the field of Neuro-Linguistic Programming (NLP) psychotherapy. The use of NLP approaches in conjunction with virtual reality (VR) therapy is one prominent trend. Immersion experiences have the potential to improve conventional NLP therapies by offering a more realistic and interesting platform for therapeutic interventions, according to research. By establishing safe spaces for therapeutic inquiry, this convergence of NLP and VR shows promise for treating a range of mental health conditions, including phobias and post-traumatic stress disorder.

The utilization of natural language processing (NLP) in individualized therapy is another noteworthy trend. Therapists are using NLP algorithms to study and comprehend the subtleties of their clients' language as technology advances, enabling a more individualized and successful therapy approach. With this individualized approach, therapists can modify their therapies according to each client's unique language preferences and patterns, resulting in psychotherapy sessions that are more focused and effective.

NOVELTIES AND PROGRESS

New developments in NLP psychotherapy are changing the field of mental health treatments. The creation of chatbot-assisted therapy based on NLP concepts is one noteworthy development. These clever chatbots are meant to mimic human-like communication and offer ongoing aid to people in need of mental health care. These chatbots, which employ natural language processing (NLP) algorithms to comprehend and react to human input, provide a scalable and easily accessible means of addressing a wide range of mental health issues.

Furthermore, combining NLP approaches with neurofeedback technology is a state-of-the-art development in psychotherapy sessions. With this combo, people can practice NLP-based activities and get immediate feedback on their neural activity. Therapists can obtain a deeper understanding of the neurological correlates of behavioral patterns and develop more focused and effective interventions by integrating neuroscience into NLP psychotherapy.

OPPORTUNITIES AND DIFFICULTIES

NLP psychotherapy has made significant progress, but there are still several issues that need to be carefully considered. A notable obstacle is the moral application of technology in therapy. As NLP applications proliferate, protecting client data privacy and security and mitigating algorithmic decision-making biases continue to be top priorities.

To preserve professional standards and preserve trust, therapists, and researchers must negotiate the ethical ramifications of using technology in psychotherapy.

Furthermore, reaching a wide range of populations is hampered by the cost and accessibility of NLP-based solutions. It is crucial to address inclusion concerns as these technologies advance to guarantee that people from a variety of socioeconomic backgrounds have fair access to cutting-edge NLP psychotherapy techniques.

Fascinating trends, cutting-edge technology, and persistent difficulties characterize the future of NLP psychotherapy. New avenues for the area are opened by the convergence of natural language processing and virtual reality, individualized therapy using NLP, and developments in chatbot-assisted and neurofeedback-enhanced therapies. To fully utilize NLP in improving psychotherapy procedures, a balanced and careful approach is necessary, as the accessibility issues and ethical considerations highlight.

www.ingramcontent.com/pod-product-compliance
Lightning Source LLC
Chambersburg PA
CBHW051921250726

48659CB00002B/771